Faith of an Unwanted Child

By: Calvin Swan
Copyrights © 2020
Euro Hoopz Academy
https://www.eurohoopz.com/
Address: South Bend, IN 46660, United States.
Email: calvinswan@eurohoopz.net
Phone: (614) 202-5842; +1 574-301-1187

Disclaimer

This book is written with the hope that you (readers) will empathize with what children go through each day, and help us secure a better future for them, as per your capacity.

The following body of work has been written as non-fiction. The events which have been portrayed by the author are expressed with the best of her knowledge and recollection. It can be asserted that all of the stories included in this book are real; there can be some names here and there and a few identifying traits which have been rendered vague so as to protect the privacy of the people involved in this narrative. All in all, it is a peek into the author's life and the emotions associated, so there is bound to be subjectivity. It is the truth comprehended by the author and not some fiction that is made up for writing this book.

Table of Contents

Author's Note

My caseworker asked me what I wanted to do, this was back when I was around 10 years of age. I wanted to work with kids. I did not know how, yet knew enough to know I wanted to make a difference. Having no one to look after you is a feeling I was rather familiar with. I knew then what I know now; I did not want these children to experience life early on the way I did.

Though I found my purpose relatively early in life, it took a while for me to plan this journey ahead. I wanted to initiate programs and facilitate children with food, clothes, and a place to bathe and sleep. The goal was to provide a secure environment where the children could be coached and mentored. I want them to experience sports. Most importantly, I want them to experience love. The idea was to create well mannered, productive citizens. The younger ages lack experience and are thus easily manipulated towards the wrong paths. They do not deserve to go to jail; they deserve to have a good job. WE DECIDE.

In 2019 I launched a non-profit organization Euro Hoopz Inc. Our Mission statement is simple: Equipping Minds, Building Bodies, and Growing Spirits. It took me a great time and effort to find the team I instinctively knew where perfect for where I was headed. I take pride in my board. It was not long before I realized that an after school program was in order. Better influence early on; leads to better people, in general.

The program that we have laid out consists of:

1. Travel Basketball Teams.

2. Open gym programs.

3. Soccer league.

4. Leadership Classes.

5. Tutoring.

6. Learning a skill.

7. Micro-business Entrepreneurship Opportunities.

We are actively seeking donations all around the globe. We have had success with many generous donations that have helped us facilitate various student batches. I need your help to raise money for the future of many children. Your generosity can not only save someone's life, but you can also change it for the better. These kids are given a platform to pursue their dream sports careers and make something out of themselves. We are constantly training them to enhance their sports skills and physical abilities.

Contribute to my cause, while I maximize my efforts to changes lives for the better.

Preface

Try not to become a person of success, but rather try to become a

person of value----**Albert Einstein**

I have known Calvin Swan for about six years. Like the rest of us, he's not a perfect person. He is, however, extremely honest, bright, very observant of human behavior and passionate about his objectives in life. Above all, he is an extremely loyal friend. He is a person of great value.

Calvin is an instantly likable individual with a warm smile and an engaging personality. He makes friends easily and, though he describes himself as an introvert, he does not come across like one. He would give a person the shirt off his back if he thought they needed it.

When I first learned about Calvin's childhood and the adolescent years, it left me in awe; how he has changed his life from horrific beginnings. He has become the complete antithesis of how he grew up. I cannot think of any other human being that I have known, who has so successfully escaped his childhood's negatives, to become the exact opposite of what he statistically should have become. In fact, it is almost miraculous that he is alive today. In this regard, he also defies the personality, psychological, and genetic studies and theories about what children would become when their childhoods are full of adverse experiences, substance abuse by their parents, and other terrible things. These are things that most of us could scarcely imagine ever happening to anyone.

He is a moral man who chooses to see the good in people no matter their race, culture, or religion. But he is also quick to know when someone is attempting to con him. He has tremendous "street intelligence," a product of being on the streets of Chicago from a very young age.

Calvin has become successful in the energy business and has a wonderful family. His desire to do good things for others and to save children from the awful events that shaped his early years is the most commendable.

Despite our huge differences in age, Calvin and I have become quite close. He sometimes calls me his father figure. In fact, just the other day, in a three-way phone conversation, he introduced me as his father. I am honored. We both share the love of basketball. I often tell him that regardless of my age, if I did not have artificial knees, I would show him how the game is played--- "school him." He laughs, doesn't believing that could happen. He's probably right, but I will not admit it anyhow.

When he asked me to help him tell his story by writing a book, I wasn't that enthusiastic. I saw it as another more task to include in the many that are crowding my retirement. But the more I learned, the more I instinctively knew that the story must be told. It must be told for several reasons. One is that Americans need to know of the horrors that some children experience in the inner city, especially black children. In that regard, perhaps it may help change racist attitudes. It also may help in his own healing experience. But far and away, the most important reason is to support his vision of helping other children avoid what happened to him and to help them grow into successful and productive members of our society.

I hope that you will read this book and take something away from it. The facts are not always pleasant, but the story is one of motivation, success, and deep, abiding hope. It can shower positivity and help people come together in their compassion, empathy, and efforts.

Kirby Whitacre.

Introduction

The first step toward success is taken when you refuse to be a captive of the environment in which you first find yourself.--Mark Caine

As I begin to write this book, I am under no illusion of it being great literature. I would not know great literature even if I saw it. I have probably only read one book in my life. I also wouldn't say that I am extremely comfortable with the skill of written language. This will be more obvious when I discuss my schooling, learning disabilities, especially in my early years. I have relied on the assistance of a good friend, to help me enhance the literature and tell my story in a readable fashion. Some of the words may not be words I would use in normal conversation, but they are, nonetheless, authentic to the events described.

This is a true story. It might not be a long one, but I hope that it will be one that will bring to your attention to the events that still occur in America, aspects clouded from the bulk of the population. I also hope that it will demonstrate the demerits that some people face since birth, though no fault of their own.

THIS is my story. It is a story that I have wanted to write for a very long time, but going back to the demons of my past was something I avoided. In doing so, I risk the further danger of having to relive memories that I have suppressed long ago. In short, my childhood was hell. Not hell in contrast to the starving children in Bangladesh. Not hell in the same sense as the child in war-torn South Sudan. But a hell that is unique to America, and one that has always been all too common in the ghettos of United States. I have been told that the very fact that I am here today, living the life that I am living, represents only a 2% statistical chance of occurring. In other words, most of my peers, or those who go through similar situations and conditions, are either dead or in far less successful standards than myself.

It has been a long, thirty-five-year road that has brought me to where I am. Though not that long, it seems so. Along the way, I encountered extreme evil and amazing good. I encountered racism, as well as compassion and acceptance. I encountered very bad people and very good people. I encountered enemies and mentors. Today, I am a husband, a father, a successful energy executive, and a man who is passionate about helping kids who like me are born into the bottom of American society. Amongst other dilemmas they face deprivations, and sometimes the depravity and vile actions of others that no child should ever have to deal with. If I can help, even a few of those children, to avoid having to deal with what I had dealt with, then my life would be a success. But frankly, I intend to help more than a few. I intend for my life to leave an imprint and set an example of what can and should be done to protect the at-risk children. For some children, childhood may never be the idyllic time that it should be, but we must never let it be the hellish existence that my siblings and I endured.

Those who treated me ill, I forgive you. I can never forget, but it does me no good to harbor resentment or hatred over something of the past. I moved on. I cannot control the past and choose not to dwell in it, even in times when memories from long ago invade my thoughts. To those who have supported me, mentored me, and loved me, I am eternally grateful. Many white people have been incredibly supportive of me. Perhaps that is the reason why I do not consider race in choosing my friends or judging those who deal with me un-ethically. I only see people. Every race has some of each. I feel completely at home in the company of white or Hispanic people as I am in the company of black people.

Regarding the initial stages of my life, make no mistake, I do not sit around feeling sorry for myself. I do not make excuses. That would accomplish nothing. Even when I sold drugs, surviving on the streets, I had quite the confidence in myself in paving my own way and did not blame those who had mistreated or abandoned me when I was a child. I did not rail against cruel fate for robbing me of my childhood, my sense of security, my time of being carefree. I did not do that because I had not experienced it and did not realize what childhood meant. I realized that I was on my own from a very young age, maybe back when I was around ten years old. So, I grew up fast, and I became a functioning adult, more than intellectual development or maturity. I may have been only ten years old, but I was already "street smart" in survival-in-the-city skills. I thought quickly, moved quickly, never stayed still long in one spot or moment in time, never trusting anyone, and knowing that my well-being was controlled by only me, despite what foster parents and caseworkers might say.

I feel that I have to share what I endured to increase awareness of the extreme obstacles blocking the path of growing up for many of America's children. These children do not start from a place equal to their peers. They are in a deep hole from the beginning, and climbing out is something that many are never able to accomplish. There is no level playing field in America, this great land of opportunity. But what I believe, what I know, is that while one person can accomplish so much, people, working together, can move mountains.

-Calvin Swan

Chapter One: The Beginning

Though no one can go back and make a brand-new start, anyone can start from now and make a brand new ending.--**Carl Bard**

I came into this world on Monday, September 12, 1983, in Chicago, Illinois, at Rush Hospital. Weather records indicate that the highest temperature that day was 73 F, and the low was 59 F. It was a cloudy Chicago day but not much wind until the evening when the maximum sustained wind for the day reached around 15 miles per hour. Visibility was listed at 20 miles. Ronald Reagan was the President of the United States. That spring, Chicago had elected its first black mayor, Harold Washington, who had defeated incumbent, Jane Byrne, in the primary before winning the general election.

I do not, of course, remember any of the above, but was curious about that day. It is my belief that humanity generally operates from an egocentric perspective, and this creates a sentimentality or nostalgia for such things as the matter above surrounding one's day of birth. People are caught up in "me" and "mine" and "I." I had to be that way while growing up, as well, because I had only myself. I hope that I have, as an adult, overcome that egocentric thought process and developed a more enlightened view of my place in the world. Certainly a more compassionate outlook toward others, without putting myself first.

There is no question that being a husband and father has helped me greatly in the process of growth, and continues to shape me as a person each and every day. I think some extremely "giving" friends, over the years, have also shown me much in that regard.

A few other minor points: my birth-date makes me a Virgo, my favorite color is red, and my favorite animal is a pit bull dog. My favorite number is 11. My favorite holiday is my Birthday. My favorite food Is rice and shrimp with vegetables. My favorite music is Nipsey hustle.

I was the second child of Calvin Swan, Sr. and Deborah Ramey. I have one older sister and four younger sisters. My parents were unmarried and very young. They were not mature enough nor financially stable enough to have children. They did not have their lives together enough to be bringing new life into the world. But those facts, of course, seldom into the equation of passion. Especially sex is an escape from the bleak realities and prospects of the ghetto. And, sometimes, people just fall in love, and it does not matter whether they are rich or poor. The problem occurs when two people, neither one equipped to be a parent, start having babies. It is, of course, the children who pay the price in those relationships. And certainly, that was the case in my family.

I do not remember my parents being around much at all. My father was a big-time drug dealer and gang-banger, and my mother was a drug-addicted teenage prostitute. We all lived in a two-story flat with my grandmother, who was my father's mother, and several other people who identified as cousins, aunts, and uncles. The memory of my deceased grandfather was of a Cuban. Cousins, aunts, and uncles lived on the top floor, my grandmother and later her boyfriend lived on the main floor, and we lived in the basement.

After my birth, the other four children followed in relatively quick succession. Our oldest sister was two years older than me, and I have no doubt that she attempted to take care of us, even though she was a toddler. She shared the same mother but had a different father.

I know that my grandmother tried to keep the entire flat of relatives together, and really my only memory of being cared for was of her. Still, I do not remember much nurturing. What occurred, in that regard, safely through infancy, I have no knowledge of or recollection. I can only assume that my grandmother, and the care of my siblings, for one another, somehow kept us all alive.

There is little doubt when it comes to reaching our developmental milestones. I would say this to be true, particularly in learning language. It is quite likely that we were all, to one extent or another, "crack babies." How much of that contributed to or caused early milestones and learning disabilities, I do not know.

Another unusual milestone would be in our potty training, where I remember being in diapers for, what I now know, have been a wholly unacceptable number of years. I also remember that diapers were sometimes only changed every few days and, in some particularly egregious cases, only once per week. The stench and squalor had become the nature of our lives, it was our reality, and we knew nothing different.

I would say that 95% of the time, or so I remember, we lived in the darl. Now I do not know whether this was because we had no electricity or for simple reasons of neglect. Again, This was our "normal."

For beds, we slept on concrete floors. During sleep or attempted sleep, we were climbed on and over by rats and roaches. They scurried here and there, without a particular fear of us. We were just part of their environment, and they were part of ours. As infants, then toddlers, and later small children, we had no concept of these creatures as unacceptable vermin that most children did not have in their lives. Sometimes we played with them. I guess you could say that rats and roaches were our pets and playmates. I suppose we also interacted and created ways to play with each other, in the dark, but we had no toys, and I really do not have much more memory. But the rats, I will remember till the end of my days.

It occurs to me that based on the "hustler" I later became, I was a little older at the time and had a wider group of peers, or perhaps even interested adults, I might have created regular cockroach races with para-mutual betting as a way of making money. Or maybe, I would have created mazes and ran some kind of gaming operation using rats or cockroaches. Of course, to an extent, I am trying to find humor for my readers, amid the pathos of such memories. But later, I will relay some of my survival skills that are not so far away from such a lifestyle, at least in terms of unwholesome and illegal activity.

Living in the dark was just one problem that we endured. There wear other problems. There was a problem with the house's sewer system, and waste frequently flooded the basement with all the attendant stench and filth that such produces. Even when this was not occurring, the smell was often present. The funny thing about smells, studies have shown that they produce some of the strongest memories, memories that last forever, and are occasionally recalled or brought back to the conscious mind by similar smells. And then one relives the events that the smells conjure. It is similar to the "diaper situation," where urine and fecal smells were what we inhaled with every breath.

I mentioned that there were no toys. There were also no birthdays or Christmas celebrations. We did not know that such things existed and were aspects of a normal childhood. When I say "normal," I mean that they are factors of the vast majority of American children's experiences. However, I must remind my readers that as dismal as what I have described maybe, we were not the only children in Chicago and elsewhere who had these experiences. Our situation was indeed terrible—but we did not know it. I have no doubt that there were others worse off, and many of those did not survive their childhoods.

You, the reader, maybe wondering about the food situation. That's a fair inquiry. To say we had food insufficiency, food insecurity, shortage of food, one could say that I am probably exaggerating towards the negative. For example, I do not remember ever having milk. To this day, I do not like and do not drink milk. The drink that we had was tap water. Water that came through old pipes in one of the poorest areas of the city.

Of course, today, there is an American scandal about lead in the water supply of many places, often places where the majority of inhabitants are black. I think it would be reasonable to assume that it is a statistically relevant possibility.

My grandmother did her best to make sure that we had some kind of food, and as often as it could be produced. We mostly had beans along with mayonnaise sandwiches, washed down by the water. To say that this fare was provided for us in abundance would not be an accurate statement. I remember being hungry, really hungry, such as most Americans have never experienced. One does not forget serious hunger, once felt.

By now, I hope you have the idea of the poverty under which we lived. As we became older and more advanced in our ability to think, our primitive survival skills kicked in. For example, when the family, or various members of the family, would visit the grocery store, we normally stole food. Back then, the question wasn't right and wrong, it was a matter of feeding the hunger. Stealing was done by adults and children. In fact, I was well below the age of five when I learned to steal food. I did it to survive. It was not something that caused me angst or created a moral dilemma—it was how I got to eat. If my developmental milestones were not met, the same could not have been said of my survival instincts, which were honed into stealthy skills at a very early age. I do not know whether I taught myself to steal by observing one of my older cousins, or even an aunt or uncle. It could have been either or a combination of both. I was not living with a flock of angels, to the say the least.

Being physically big for my age, as I grew older, I took it upon myself to steal food for my sisters and myself. I was bigger and a sort of a protector for my siblings.

I was good at stealing. Preoccupation with getting food was a dominant thought during my days and reinforced at night while laying hungry on a concrete floor. Looking back on those times, I am, in some ways, surprised that eating rats and cockroaches never occurred to me. But then, again, they were playmates and a part of my environment. I suppose it would have taken a more advanced kicking-in of my primitive survival skills to get me to skin a rat.

As I reflect back upon those early years of childhood, I realize that almost all of the influences I had received were negative in nature. My grandmother, however, was an exception. But other than that, I was exposed to a few examples of compassion, ethical, moral, or even legal behavior, to shape the development of what could be called my conscience. Such values are often absent when living in abject poverty.

I will again mention how seldom we saw my parents, and it wasn't as if they' were paragons of moral virtue.

A minor point that I have failed to mention, one you might have assumed by this point, is related to hygiene as we grew older and came out of our diapers. Baths or showers were not an occurrence that, in any way, could be described as regular events. There were no teeth brushing. I will leave it to the reader to think about other daily or regular hygiene matters by simply saying, whatever it was, we did not do it, we did not have it, and it was not a part of our routine or our consciousness. Visits to the dentist? Eye doctor? Regular doctor? Nope, no way.

During those times, when my grandmother would bring us upstairs to her quarters, it was like another world, a novelty, a vacation trip. She tried to do that often, and those were the times that we got some sense of family, of normalcy. Even that lacked by common standards, but for us, it was a treat. It was, perhaps, during those times that we had the experience of feeling loved. A person cannot develop a true sense of self-worth unless they have some experience of the expression of love.

As I got older, I moved around after living in the flat and gained more contact with all the relatives living there. I had my first experiences of witnessing sex, as in walking in on my mother with a "John" and my first experience of looking at drug consumption. As I mentioned before, sex

15

is one way to escape the realities of the ghetto, and drugs are certainly also at the top of the list of coping mechanisms. Of course, using drugs, or prostituting, have serious health and moral consequences, and what I would call consequences of the soul. Both can be lethal. But sometimes there seems to be no other way to escape. It all becomes a vicious reoccurring reality. In fact, when repeated often enough, these behaviors take on a sort of normalcy that further obfuscates any morals or ethics.

It goes without saying that a child under eight or nine years should not go through the experience of stealing, or of witnessing sex or drug usage. If such things confuse the psyche of the perpetrator, what can they do to the child?

I do not tell my readers these things for sympathy. I do not need pity. I simply want people to understand that such a life is not uncommon. It happened just as I have described, and I cannot change the past. I can only seek to remediate the effects that it had upon me and how I was shaped as an individual by the events that I have described.

If, in precisely because of the things that happened to me, that was my reality, that I have such a desire to help children and the youth of today. May they be spared what my siblings and I endured.

By this point, I suppose there are some people who are left shaking their heads at the horrific events and conditions I have described. All these years later, having learned what normal children experience, I look upon some of these memories as surreal. How could they have happened? And yet, they did happen and are ingrained indelibly in my memory. It would be bad enough if nothing else happened in my childhood other than the already described, but as you will see in the next chapter, things only got worse.

Chapter Two: Tragedy

Out of suffering have emerged the strongest souls; the most massive characters are seared with scars.

-Khalil Gibran

In spite of our deprivations, we somehow managed to survive. When I was around seven, my youngest sister came along. She was the final baby, and due to the events about to unfold, a sister that I know the least of all my siblings.

As I said, the older that I got, the more my interactions increased with the other inhabitants of our flat, cousins, aunts, uncles, and numerous visitors that came and went by at all hours of the day and night. The place was always alive with activity. And, a great deal of the activity was illegal. Things like prostitution, drug dealing, and usage.

Let me again remind the reader that despite the fact that I was aware of these activities, I did not necessarily know that they were bad, illegal, or whatever the terminology was. They were simply basic activities of the house. I suppose some of these I did not understand at first. But I probably gained a better understanding as time went on, and as I was exposed more and more.

Unfortunately, food continued to be an issue into those years, and to obtain something to eat, in any way necessary, was seldom far from our minds. Likewise, the increased interaction with my relatives proved to be bad. In fact, my food insecurity, coupled with my increased relationship with one of my aunts, was to develop into an outrageous case of child abuse.

When I was about seven years old, my aunt had set up a regulation upon me, with which I had to comply, or no food. Quite simply, I had to have sex with her before I was allowed to have food. Now, as I previously stated, I had seen people having sex before this, but that does not mean that I wanted to have sex or had any inkling as to the particulars of such an act... In fact, it was an ordeal for me and one which no child should have to experience. I was told to never tell anyone about this frequent ritual, or something bad would happen to me. Therefore, I never did, at least at the time, tell anyone. Besides, I wanted to eat.

But I was not the only one to suffer in such a fashion. While my aunt was abusing me, my uncle was abusing some of my sisters in a similar fashion.

As I look back on and remember the abuse now, I just sort of sit quietly, gazing blankly off into the sky and ponder on these events quietly and without much emotion, mostly feeling numb. It all seems surreal, but the truth is that it happened and that I was helpless. I was helpless to save myself or save my sisters.

I can only imagine what someone reading these accounts, someone who has never remotely experienced anything like this, thinks. I assume the reaction to be one of shock and surprise. As for me, I now know that events like these are rare than I thought as a child. But we must all remember that my sisters and I were not the only ones to ever suffer this kind of abuse, or even worse. That's the whole point.

Such was the abusive, dysfunctional, and ill-fated family, into which we had been born, had to endure childhood, and had to survive. All of these, amongst other things, contributed to me growing into and becoming a very angry young man, who acted out, stole things, and who ultimately learned that selling drugs was a way to get easy money and lots of it. I will discuss it further in the chapters to come.

I think I have made it clear by this point that if there was any love, any sanity, any bit of nurturing in my life, it came from my fraternal grandmother, Lillie. She was a Christian woman and was known to pray or sing, even quite loudly, and even during the night. But she was also a practical woman. For example, her bedroom door was much more like a jail gate. She had this installed because many members of this large extended family stole from her room, mostly money. I have to admit that there were times when she was at church, I had gone into her room and stolen her peppermints, which I sold around the neighborhood.

So, finally, she did the practical thing. Once she retired at night, she was essentially shut away in her citadel, having given herself hours. She has done her best, with almost no money, to keep this large extended family together each and every day. I suppose the door had behind it

20

other reasons and that probably related to all the people who came and went, and all the night-time activities of the house. Grandma Lilly could at least be certain that she was safe and secure in her room once she retired for the evening.

On Saturday, October 20, 1991, around 7:30 in the evening, unimaginable tragedy struck. I was in the kitchen, where my grandmother had just given me some beans to eat. We talked, and then she went to her room and locked "the gate" behind her. I continued eating beans but was soon interrupted by the smell of smoke. By this time, I heard screams and yelling all over the house, as my various relatives fled without so much as a check on us kids.

I pounded my little eight-year-old fist on my grandmother's gated door and yelled, "Smoke!" Or maybe, "fire!" I then hurried to the basement and got my sisters moving upstairs. My oldest sister was not at home, but my next oldest sister and I grabbed and carried our younger sisters upstairs and out of the house.

By this time, the neighbors had been alerted, the police and fire department were arriving, and then came an ambulance or, perhaps, multiple ambulances. Apparently, everyone was out of the house except my grandmother and her boyfriend, Nate. Soon there was a huge explosion as the furnace blew up the entire house, shaking the neighborhood as if a bomb exploded. My recollection is that we had not been out of the house for even a minute. We children were hurried by various first responders into police cars or ambulances.

I probably do not need to explain to the terror that this event bought. The smoke, the fire, the explosion, the police and firefighters everywhere, neighbors running over as close as they dared. Our family had scattered throughout the emergency vehicles. It was chaos. It was a great deal for children to comprehend. I was, at eight years old, the oldest of my siblings present there.

We were taken to a hospital where we were kept for the rest of the night, safe and together. However, at some point in confusion, either before or after we got to the hospital, we learned of the death of our grandmother and of Nate. We were shaken, confused, and some of us were completely inconsolable. For, whatever we had been through, whatever had happened, or whatever had been denied in our young lives, we still very much loved our grandmother. She was the one constant, the one familiar and mutually loved face in our lives.

As I explained, the rest of the extended family, who were residents of the flat, had been the first to escape. I do not remember any of them helping my siblings, although some may have been yelling warnings to get out of the house. The cause of the fire attributed to my uncle, smoking crackdown in our section of the basement. While using crack, he got a blanket or sheet, too close to the exposed flame at the bottom of the furnace. The furnace had recently been worked on, and as my grandmother had little money, it had been done on the cheap. It seemed that the contractor may have left some faulty wiring issues. Nevertheless, the main cause was my uncle's crack usage.

I am quite certain that most of the relatives who lived in the flat with us, do not want this book to be written and parts of the story told. In fact, I have kept secret most of the awful things that I have described, from most of the people in my life. My wife did not even learn of some of these events until we had been married for many years. Keeping such things to oneself can indeed be a burden. I doubt it is ever a good thing to do. I am sure there is a psychological toll to be paid for my doing.

I am not out to punish those relatives or to cause them any trouble or either drag them through the mud by a book, no matter what they did to my sisters or me. But, by the same token, I am no longer hiding the truth of those terrible events or keeping them to myself. What happened should not have happened, and it is not my job to keep the family secrets or to attempt to keep the peace by letting the memories be contained within the constraints of my mind. I will suffer no longer. I choose to no longer be a victim but to take back control of my life and live with the dignity that was stolen from me when I was just a defenseless child. If the perpetrators deny my story, or "cannot remember," I assume that is for a reason, but ultimately they will have to answer for their actions, not to me but to a greater power.

You may recall when I mentioned that the relatives who lived in the flat were my father's relatives. After the fire, we children ended up in the projects, in the care of my mother's people. Oddly, or ironically, my mother's mother, my grandmother, was also named Lilly.

Chapter Three: The Projects

Poverty is the worst form of violence---**Mahatma Gandhi**

After the fire, we children were given to the custody of our mother, who immediately remanded us to the custody of her mother, Lillian, illegally. We now lived in what was called "the Projects," a complex called Rockwell Gardens. Therein lies the paradox. Rockwell Gardens sounds like a wonderful place, nice name, conjuring up visions of a green garden. Nothing could be further from the truth. The Projects were the epitome of ghetto living by definition. There was a great deal more concrete than grass and greenery. Thousands of people crammed into the space of a building or several buildings. They are whole towns in rural Midwest America with fewer people than there were in my building. Like other complexes, Rockwell Gardens was a government-subsidized shelter. In other words, the cheapest housing available.

Such conditions, with poor people in such proximity, inevitably leads to troubles such as stealing, fighting, drinking, drugs, and shootings. Violence was nothing but an everyday event. The police were omnipresent. Our neighbors were taken away and arrested almost every day. Depravity, depression, despair, hopelessness, anger, all abounded. Our complex, like many others, gained a reputation that I am sure surpassed that of Dodge City, Kansas, in the 1870s. In fact, I am told that in terms of violence and police repulsion, we were exceeded only by a complex called Cabrini Green (another nice name). One or the other, or both complexes, were in the news daily for acts of crime and violence.

Our building was of thirteen stories with apartments crammed full of families, extended families, sometimes even strangers. They all lived closely together and almost always, with way too many people in one apartment. At first, we lived on the first floor and later the third. We were six kids, a grandmother, two aunts, and an uncle. We had three rooms and a bathroom with a tub and no shower.

None of the adults were working at that time. We all survived on my grandmother's social security check and food stamps. Food was scarce and usually consisted of cereal, noodles, ravioli, etc. These were items that could be easily prepared, stretched out, and used to fill hungry stomachs in lieu of well-balanced meals. And, of course, they were cheap.

In terms of an actual indoor environment, our new living quarters were not that different from our previous residence. We were cramped together, slept on concrete floors, and our familiar pets, cockroaches, and rats were in abundance.

If what I have described so far sounds awful, I would say, "No, it wasn't. It was hell." But again, it was what we had to deal with, it was our everyday reality.

I loved my grandmother, just as I loved my other grandmother. And my fondest memories of both are the talks that we had, one on one. As I said, both were named Lillian, or Lilly. The new one was ill with diabetes and high blood pressure, she spent most of her time in bed. She was not religious like my other grandmother, but, like my other grandmother, she did treat me well.

Again, we had no birthdays and no Christmas. I do not remember my aunts and uncle ever giving us anything. In fact, one of my aunts would go so far as to hide food from us. In animal packs like wolves, for example, the young and the weak eat last, if there are any leftover. I guess that is sort of the way it was in our family. The oldest and strongest were entitled, by their size and power, to the food. Never-mind, growing, and developing children. I have to wonder, where was the morality, the compassion, the human decency, the care of family members, for one another. If you have the impression that I had no relationship with my parents, and have no good feelings for my aunts and uncles, then my attempt to write is a successful one indeed.

And so, for two or three years, I cannot remember exactly, Rockwell Gardens was our home. We children did not go to school. In one respect, we were like anonymous individuals or people without a country. All of our paperwork and identifications had burned up in the fire, and we had no records to verify our existence. None of the adults with whom we lived had the wherewithal, or the desire, to correct this or to see that we got an education.

So, there I was, at eight years old, I began to run totally "amuck." I was my own person. I did whatever I wanted. I came and went when and where I pleased, be it day or night. There were no particular disciplines. I often went out yet encouraged my sisters to stay inside. I was very protective of them, as I was quite aware of the outside violence.

When I went out, I engaged in whatever unwholesome activity I could find. Throwing rocks, stealing, vandalism, and so forth. I was a sort of "junior resident" of the same ilk as many of the adults in Rockwell Gardens.

It was during this time that I figured out that I could make money, and a great deal of money, by my standards, by selling drugs. And so, I, along with some of my young friends, had our own sort of local cartel, selling crack. We were initially extended some credit by those higher up in the drug business. We paid up when we sold our product. I found out of a talent that still persists to this day, the ability to sell. My market was ready-made; it was the crack-heads living in the complex. They came to me once word got out that I sold. I did not really have to work too hard to expand my business.

It has been pointed out to me that my history as a drug dealer was unusual, as I was never a user. Oh, later on, I smoked a little marijuana, but basically, I never did drugs or alcohol. I always felt that it was important to keep my wits and be able to think quickly and move even quicker. There were plenty of dangers, not so much from crackheads, as much from gangs and others who would have no problem beating me or stealing from me. I never cheated anyone in a drug deal, and I always treated my clients with respect. In that regard, I never felt anyone of my associates, suppliers, or clients was coming to get me because I had pimped them over. Oddly, in an illegal business, I had a certain code of honor.

By selling drugs, I was able to buy food, which I always shared with my sisters. As my business expanded, I was able to buy some clothes as well. I often had $40 or $50 in my pocket. As an eight-year-old living in abject poverty, that was a fortune.

From time to time, I would buy my grandmother things. She liked pickled pigs feet to eat and gin to drink. I did not have to convince any adults to buy booze for me, nor did I have to find and buy it on a black market, where the cost would be much better, because of my age and inability to get it any other way. No, I bought it in stores. The storekeepers in the neighborhood sold it directly to me, with no questions asked; cash and carry. Eight years old comes in, produces the cash, and buys gin.

My mother never came around much. She was too busy on the streets and too far along in the spiral of horrific drug addiction. Whether her addiction was obvious to me and contributed to my abstinence from drugs, I cannot say, but it is certainly possible. I had seen enough people using to be well aware of the effects of long-term usage.

As time passed, I guess we kids had become too much of a responsibility. My aunts and grandmother called the Illinois Department of Children and Family Services. They came to the apartment to take us away. I think my grandmother regretted making that phone call the minute she opened the door, while the workers identified themselves and their reason for coming to our apartment. I am positive she did, once she saw the fear in our eyes as the crying and howls of protest began.

We were taken first to a facility where we were questioned extensively about our identities and so forth. In a short time, we were separated, put into foster homes. The younger children were stabilized in foster homes more quickly and later, adoptions. After many foster homes, my two oldest sisters and I were placed in a group home.

During this time, my mother continued her activities, and my father was shot. The result of being a heavy gang banger and drug dealer. He recovered and was eventually sent to prison for armed robbery. I think with his previous time in prison and the sentence this time, he amassed over twenty years of total prison time.

Chapter Four: The System

You are free to make whatever choices you want, but you are not free from the consequences of those choices---**Anonymous**

So, upon leaving the Projects, I became a ward of the State of Illinois. This happened because technically, after the fire, we kids were actually given to our mother, and she was expected to care for us. Instead, it was she who placed us with her mother, Grandma Lilly. So, once DCFS was called, the court ruled that my mother was guilty of abandonment, and we kids became wards of the State of Illinois.

The younger girls, being young and cute, went to a few foster homes and were adopted. We, the oldest three children, were placed in a number of foster homes. The people who take children into their homes to foster are paid by the State for doing so. So, while I suppose some have an altruistic intention, most do it for the money.

I was probably shifted to over twenty foster homes in the next year or two. Sometimes shifting occurs because of the influx of new children into the system, while those already in the system are moved along. However, changes were often caused by my own behavior, which was angry and defiant. After all, I came from an environment lacking discipline, where I could come and go at my will. Now, I had adults telling me what move to make. Sometimes they hid food from me. That brought up some of my old issues and experiences. Often they were mean and rough in their treatment of me. Sometimes they were abusive, but never sexually as I had previously experienced. When I became defiant or ran away, I usually ended up in a new foster home. I eventually adopted the habit of keeping my bags packed at all times, to be ready for my next move, or sometimes, for the next opportunity to run away.

During all of these moves, I was in an out of several schools. I would often skip, but in general, my attendance was somewhat regular. However, having not attended previously, and because of all the developmental milestones that were delayed in my upbringing, I did not do well in school.

Ultimately, my two oldest sisters and I were placed in the same group home. It was a lot like being a jail for children, with windows that only opened a couple of inches, just too barely allow in some air. Doors that were of metal and heavy to keep us locked in. However, it was three meals a day and no rats or roaches. Plus, seeing my sisters regularly was a comfort.

The group home system housed kids ages 7 to 17, and when one turns 18, they were put into independent living or released from the system altogether.

A huge difference was that the two of us had a room, and we actually had our own beds. This was a major change in my life, but I did not appreciate it as much as one would think. Primarily because it came at the price of giving up my independence. Remember, I had been functioning with adult-like freedoms when I lived at Rockwell Gardens.

Also, we had medical care. Which was a nice change. We settled in at one school, Cleveland Elementary. Suddenly, life was more stable, more regular, and more routine. But, being angry and defiant, I managed to get into trouble in the group home and at school. Trouble in the group home meant the loss of privileges. This usually meant not playing on the basketball team, which I had made. We also had birthdays and Christmas celebrations at the group home, which could also be taken away in case of negligent behavior.

While I attended school fairly regularly, I often skipped. This, of course, had repercussions at home in terms of restricting my fun activities. I did not do well in school, partially because I was discovered to have a learning disability but also due to my previously limited and inconsistent schooling.

In the home, I got into fights all the time with other kids. This often led to the loss of privileges and restrictions on movement.

While at home, I worked in the kitchen, the first physical labor job I ever had. I got paid a small amount every two weeks for this work. Since regular meals were no longer an issue, I used this money to purchase drugs to sell. I sold these in the home and at school. But I continued my policy of not being a user, except occasionally smoking marijuana. Since

33

my drug market was now mostly kids and not adults, I could not sell as much crack as I did before, but I sold some. My business now involved marijuana, but the margins of profits were much less than those of selling crack.

I kept my drugs safe from room inspections by cutting a hole in my mattress and securing the drugs there or by sleeping with them in my underwear. Room searches were random and unpredictable. My methods served me fairly well.

I also made a few escape attempts from the group home, but escape was easier during the coming and going to school on a school day. During these times, the police were called. Once caught, I would be taken to a sort of juvenile detention home for a period of days, before being taken back to the group home, where I had certain activities taken away as punishment.

Sometimes, while getting into a fight or more severe behavior issues at home, the police would be called to the home to handle the situation. However, it was not unusual for the staff to handle such situations, and sometimes they did so somewhat aggressively, probably out of frustration, to counter the negative behaviors that were all too frequently exhibited by the home's residents.

On one occasion, I had my teeth run through my lip by a 6'7" inch, 245-pound staff member. I thought I was a tough guy, but there was no way to be more physical than someone so big. I do not remember whether his force was justified. It may not have been. I could be a problem and fairly consistently so. I am sure that I thought it was just another case of an adult being mean to a kid, which only reinforced my primitive view that life is controlled by the biggest and strongest, or in some cases, the ones with weapons.

But there is no question, as I mentioned previously, that staff in homes get very frustrated with the constant negative behavior of the residents. It is quite difficult for anyone to keep their cool in such situations.

Once, I was discovered to have a gun in my possession. I had purchased it on the streets with my drug profits. I even had a few, what I would call a "minor shootout," with other street individuals, while in possession of the gun. However, I was taken by police to the juvenile detention home on that occasion as on others when I would run away.

At home, there were nice staff members and some who were not. But overall, despite regular meals, a nice bed, a warm room, and seeing my sisters, I did not like the group home. As I said, I felt like it was a jail for kids, and I missed my accustomed, almost total freedom that I once had.

One of the very worst requirements of the group home, in my view, was regular mental health therapy and regular meetings with a case manager. I am an introvert and did not like being forced to answer questions about myself, questions that I considered stupid, and about my personal business, not that of anyone else. Also, failure to participate meant loss of activities. So, forced mental health therapy was another thing that pissed me off.

As an adult, I can certainly look back and see why therapy was part of the program. A popular acronym these days is "ACES." This stands for *Adverse Childhood Experiences,* and there is no question that everyone who lived in that group home had suffered many ACES in their young lives. I know I had. But it would be years into the future before I could understand fully and come to terms with just how bad my childhood was. Still, forced mental health therapy was an ordeal for me, one that had to be endured in order to get to do some of the things I wished to do.

Chapter Five: The Streets

Freedom is not the right to live as we please, but the right to find out how we ought to live in order to fulfill our potential.**-Ralph Waldo Emerson**

I think that many people have heard about black athletes, musicians, and others who grew up "in the Hood," or survived the "ghetto," or managed to make it "on the streets." Well, these are "certainly" terms that could be used to describe me. I once had to explain to a good friend that I think so fast, and am so impatient with people, and am also on the move so much, because they were learned skills for survival when I literally was on the streets.

So the streets provided me with skills of survival. Another is the ability to quickly read people and judge them. I think my ability in this area is outstanding, But I would admit that no one and no skill are perfectly honed. For example, I never saw anything negative from the man who got me involved with his church, as I will relay elsewhere, and then stole my money and clothes. I never saw that coming, but in general, I think I have been a pretty good judge of people and pretty quick to size them up.

Not all things learned on the streets are good. Which is obvious as I sold drugs and carried a gun. Also, a person can develop paranoia about enemies seen and unseen. One can begin to feel that someone is out to get you. One easily loses the ability to trust. A person loses track of the righteousness that exists in some parts of humanity. One learns to avoid the police and to fear them, that they are predators that must be outwitted. And so, a great deal of the mindset that develops after a long period of living on the streets is negative, and one might say, harmful to the soul.

The above might sound a little strange to someone who grew up in the middle class or even upper class, "white America." I think that for a great number of young black men, it is just the reality of life. It is a reality that all too often ends their lives prematurely. For others, who do not die or get killed, it nevertheless scars them in a way from which they may never really recover. So, they become drug-addicted, perpetrators of a lifetime of petty, or not so petty, crimes. They lose all hope and get beaten down into despair, spending entire lifetimes in the ghetto, never knowing that there is a better world than the one in which they found themselves at a young age.

At the age of eighteen, I was let out of the system. I could not wait. Part of the deal involved my father, Calvin, Sr. getting out of prison on parole. The deal required my father to stay out of Chicago, where it was too much temptation and trouble. He was to build a home where we would both live. My father had a friend, a wealthy white friend, who actually behaved more like a caseworker or someone going the extra mile for my father as he got him out of prison. I have no idea how they met or how their relationship came together, but this wealthy white entrepreneur secured a house for my father, and I went to live there. It was almost as if both of us were on parole, kinda like we both had gotten out of prison, and were being set up in a house, in the distant suburbs, in order to re-start our lives.

The situation went to real south quick. My father was telling me what to do and trying to control me while I developed new friends and new markets for drugs. Also, he would slip into Chicago to see a young lady regularly.

I had learned to drive while still in the group home. A friend and mentor of one of my uncles had taught me and saw to it that I got my license. As I was always frugal with money and saved much of what I made from my drug dealing, I had enough money to buy my first car shortly after getting out of the system. Through the subsequent years, I went through many cars, paying cash for all. One of my first cars crapped out because I did not know of simple maintenance facts, such as regularly changing the oil. But no matter, I just bought another one.

Through the help of his friend and or his actual parole officer, my father got a job at a local college working in maintenance.

Our arrangement lasted all of about six or seven months, till I had enough of his control, and moved out. For a short time, I lived with my father's rich white friend. He had lots of famous visitors who came to his home. One night at dinner, the guest was one of the most famous evangelists in American history. But at the time, I had no idea who this man really was.

The relationship with my father's rich friend soon soured as he tried to indulge himself too much into my business, probably in an effort to help me stay on the straight and narrow. But I would not have it. So, I moved out, and for a long time, lived in my car, or with friends, or occasionally with girls that I met. I had a few clothes, and I used laundromats to keep them clean. I played basketball in gyms and took my showers there. All the while, I was developing a low key---but high income, drug business in the suburbs all around Chicago. I was back to dealing with cocaine exclusively.

Almost as a cover, I was going to high school, changing schools regularly, and as will be described elsewhere, attempting to play basketball.

Somewhere along the line, I became best friends with a Mexican who shared my occupation of drug dealing. We had three other Mexican and a black friend, who frequently hung out with us. We kind of went between Chicago and the suburbs for our business. I continued my mobile living style, except that sometimes I stayed with my friend.

The six of us were a relatively close-knit group of friends, and I enjoyed their company a good bit. We all had a mutual trust over each other and were of similar ages.

One night my best friend wanted to attend a party in Chicago at someone's house. He had it in his mind to see this girl that he had met. She apparently knew he was a drug dealer and was doing well. This may have been because he was a flashy dresser, lots of jewelry, and so forth. I feel that she may have set up the events that occurred that evening.

We went to the party by car and parked in the alley behind the house. The party had been going on already for an hour or so. So we went in and, at first, everything seemed cool, we were not there to sell drugs but to chill and have a good time. The girl that my friend was interested in was there. Everything was going fine until suddenly someone shut off the lights. At that point, people started shooting their guns off inside the house and in the dark.

My friend and I were completely disconcerted by this change of events, and ran out of the house and to the alley, to get our car and escape. By the time we got to our car, several armed and masked young men were there. One held a gun to my head while another held a shotgun on my friend. They demanded of our drug money. That night, by our standards, we really did not have much money on us, maybe around $200 in total. This angered them, and before I knew it, my friend was shot with the twelve-gauge shotgun and killed instantly. The thug holding a gun to my head, pulled the trigger, it misfired, and angrily, he knocked me over the head as the sound of police sirens were near. I was out cold. Due to the shots fired earlier in the home, the police were already on their way.

I was taken to a hospital emergency room and questioned extensively by the police. However, I did not know our assailants, who, as I said, had masks. We did not have drugs or were not making a deal, and so there was little I could say to be of help to the police. Honestly, I never felt good about talking to the police. I was released and never saw my friend again. I did not attend his funeral. I know that this event, perhaps more than any other in my life, had a profound effect on me--- it changed me in ways that were not immediately obvious at the time. Some of these may still be playing out. It was not just a "wake-up call'; it was life-changing. My thoughts kept returning over and over to my friend and to those events, and all these years later, they still do.

As for the other members of our group who were not with us that night, all were later killed except one, who committed suicide in jail.

The immediate future followed me starting my college odyssey, which is described elsewhere in this book. Attending college was really a cover for drug dealing, but also to seek an opportunity in college basketball. At one point, I even took a job in a nursing home or retirement center to cover my drug dealing activities.

During this time, I continued to live with many friends, a few days here and there. Most were white, and my college attendance and nursing home job were to give me credibility in their eyes so they could not suspect me of drug dealing and call the police. I was living a lie and covered it well.

About this time, I met a drug dealer who became a sort of mentor to me. He asked me if I wanted to be a successful dealer or a gangster, much like my father. Gangsters get shot, and they go to prison, so obviously, I didn't want that.

So, his advice to me was to sell drugs only in the suburbs and stay out of the city. In the suburbs, I would deal with white people mostly, people well-off, who did not carry guns around and were not likely to rob or shoot me. In the city, I was a target and would always need to be armed (which I frequently was) and always be on my guard. But mostly, in the city, my clientele would be a lower class group, less money for me, and lots more risk. So, I took the advice to heart and concentrated solely on the suburban market for the drugs. I sold to judges, doctors, lawyers, teachers, and other professionals, mostly white people. I made a great deal of money, much more than I would have made in the city and much more safely. I kept low key, and by my cover of the job and my college, I never attracted any police attention.

One other event happened about this time in a small town in Illinois. I met a white man who befriended me and got me involved in his church. I had never been particularly involved with a church, but remember, I was also not a drug user nor a drinker. I didn't consider the evils of my business. It was, as was said in the Godfather movies, "strictly business."

43

I considered myself a businessman and treated everyone with respect. So, I had respect for this supposed friend and attended his church. In the end, he stole all my money and all my clothes!

Chapter Six: Basketball

"Basketball season is that time of year around which all biological life revolves."

-Kareem Abdul Jabbar

Many people have in their lives, something besides just the people that they care about, stuff that they are passionate about, what fulfills them, something they are really good at. It may be a vocation, an avocation, music, drawing, art, sports, poetry, a particular subject at school, video games, cards, or many other things, often creative endeavors. When one finds in himself such a personal talent, it often becomes a part of that person's life in a special way. It becomes how they identify themselves and how others choose to label them. It becomes almost inseparable from the person. Often it is something creative or something good for the soul, something that takes them away from their problems and gives them release. It can make them feel special.

For me, that passion, that talent, was basketball. I do not know when I had first bounced a ball or saw someone doing so, and wanting to emulate it. I assume that growing up in Chicago, in the era of the Bulls NBA Championships, had been a huge influence on me subconsciously or otherwise.

No child starts off being magically good at basketball. Nevertheless, I do believe that the game comes to those who are what we call "naturals." Indeed, it takes a great deal of hard work to get polished. But I believe in the old adage that "you can take ten young people off the street, and if they want to 'hit' and be aggressive, they can become football players. But basketball players are born." Now I know that other athletes would take exception in me saying this. But the fact is that basketball requires innate coordination, quickness, thought process, balance, core strength, timing, rhythm, and hand-eye coordination, which must be mastered thoroughly in order to be good. And to my way of thinking, players are born with these traits to be developed, while others who do not possess them can do all the work and practice they want, and still cannot become good basketball players. If that is arrogant, I am sorry, but this is what I truly believe.

Of course, I think of basketball as a special game. It has been a big part of who I am. I still play three times a week, and I spent a good part of the last summer working out with professional teams in Spain. It releases me from all my problems and allows my creativity to flow into the performance of the game. It is, as has been said, "Poetry in motion." Let me put it another way, in words which others have said, Basketball is not a matter of life and death. It is much more important than that". Okay, enough of my hyperbolic statements. But I say these to the stress of my unabashed love for the game.

Like bouncing a ball, I do not know how old I was when I shot my first shot, but I do remember that a man named DJ, gave me my initial introduction to the game. He was a staff member at my group home. I was an angry young man of thirteen years of age. He, very wisely, determined that "playing ball" might be a way to help me control my anger or at least release some of it in such a physical activity. Neither he, nor anyone else, actually taught me the game, but I will forever be grateful for his insight on introducing me to it.

I began to play whenever I was angry. Then, I began to play at other times. I started to really enjoy the activity but mostly played by myself. I cannot overly stress this as another positive of the game; it can be played alone and without much equipment.

After a time, I realized or else thought that I was getting pretty good. So, I tried out for the home team and made the squad. This led me to try out for the elementary school team, and again, made the squad. However, the elementary coach did not play me, and to this day, I believe it was because I came from a group home. This made me angry, I quit and did not play again for two or three more years. During those years, I reverted to continue being a very angry young man and often got into trouble, probably more often than not.

Eventually, I could not resist trying out for my high school team, which I later made. However, my style of play did not suit the coach. Now I can look back and understand that despite my talent, I had been taught no concept of "team," either offensively or defensively. I honed my game individually, alone for hours on end. Playing effectively with teammates, using team fundamentals and strategy, was something of which I had no experience. With that said, I also believe there existed an inherent bias against kids from group homes or kids who were in "the system." And, I certainly had a record of getting into trouble, causing problems, and being angry. Those factors were well known and were not in my favor either.

Before long, I met a new friend and began attending the open gym at his school. Later, I transferred there. The same pattern followed all over again, making the team, but not really suiting the coach. In all, for basketball and other reasons having to do with moving within the system, I went to six different schools and, as a result, never got to play a game of high school basketball. In retrospect, I can see that my temper and my personality probably played a significant role in all of this, as did my actual style of play. Because if a player is good, then a decent coach can help him or her change the way they play, and also understand strategy. But, this would have required a great deal of change and work on my part, and I did not possess that level of patience. Additionally, I was not a good student in the classroom. So, basketball is a cerebral game, I was unwilling to adopt that discipline to enhance my level of play.

I have no doubt that I graduated from high school just to get rid of me. I could not read at the required standard, I was not proficient in my subjects, and my attendance was abysmal. Add all that to my disciplinary record, and graduating me was the course that my final high school settled upon.

After high school, I found out that I could go to college freely because I had been a ward of the state. I decided to go to junior college, the College of Du Page. I thought I would attempt to make the basketball team as a walk-on. I tried out and did, in fact, make the team. However, in an old familiar refrain, the coach didn't play me—not for the entire season. He displayed a biased behavior to others on the team, and frankly, I considered his style of coaching as abrupt. Some of this was probably my ego talking and also because of a lack of inexperience with discipline.

Going to college for free was all well and good, but I still needed money to survive. And so, I did what I did best, I sold drugs and made it off fairly well. Things not working out, academically, or with basketball, I left school at the end of the semester.

Sometime after that, I met a friend who was going to Louisiana Monroe for college. I decided to go with him and get out of the Chicago area. This venture lasted for less than a semester as I decided not to play basketball anymore, I was making a small fortune selling drugs. My name as a drug dealer had got around, and the police were closing in on me, so I felt it best to leave the college and the state.

Sometime later, I found my way to Triton College, repeating my same old pattern: making the team, not playing, selling drugs, not going to class, and finally quitting the team. One of my friends there was from Michigan, the Kalamazoo area. He said he knew some of my family members that lived there. These were people I had not known, but I decided to go there.

In Kalamazoo, I met my future wife, an extremely beautiful and intelligent young lady named LaDawn White. I will relay more about her in another chapter. For now, I want to continue discussing my basketball journey.

After leaving basketball alone for a couple of years, I ended up in Ohio, attempting to play professional basketball. I tried out and made the team, sort of a semi-pro or minor league basketball. Ultimately I ended up leading the league in scoring. While there, I was staying with various people and in my car. I was attempting to save money to get a film of my plays to send to an agent so that he could get me on a professional team overseas. I was hoping to eventually get a tryout with the minor league that later became the NBA Development League. I thought, or hoped, against all hope, that I might end up at the Cleveland Cavaliers.

In the end, my team never paid me anything, and the entire process of striving to get high-level tryouts, dealing with agents, etc., seemed "political" and majorly based on a known reputation (as in having been a college star, which I was not, and who one knew). I was left dully demoralized and fed up. I returned to Kalamazoo, concentrating on building a family, giving up playing basketball, and taking up training youngsters in the game.

As I mentioned at the beginning of the chapter, I still play basketball three times a week. This is a diverse group of friends who play early in the morning. I would play even more if there were more opportunities. Again, as I previously mentioned, last summer, I was in Spain with a business colleague and ended up working with some professional teams. I suppose the dream never ends. Despite being almost 35 years old and not having played organized basketball for many years, I did attract some contractual interest. However, the salary was not substantial enough to uproot my family. My wife has a budding business in childcare, and I did not wish to disrupt it. Additionally, it would have put a temporary hold on my goal of getting a youth program, of many dimensions, going in South Bend.

This was a tough call for me, but in the end, I believe I made the right decision. Still, I cannot help but wonder what I might have accomplished.

I have included this chapter on basketball because, without it, my reader could not fully understand me, where I've been, and who I am. Basketball is at the very core of my being. It is intertwined in the very fabric of my life. I suppose that all sounds grandiose or somewhat like the language of a much more classic or higher quality literature. Nevertheless, it expresses basketball's part in my life.

Kareem Abdul Jabbar once said, that "Basketball season is that time of year around which all biological life revolves." I have no idea if anyone else understands this the way that Kareem meant it, but I do, I really do.

It is my belief that there is a group youth who feel the same and that basketball might just be the tool by which I can help them change their lives and move them in the right direction for a brighter future. I have had this idea, this goal of beginning a program, one unique in scope, for some time. I believe the time has come to make it a reality.

Finally, I want to add that I am keenly aware of some inherent dangers that use basketball as a tool with the youth. It is regarded as the game of the inner city, with black kids everywhere playing all the time. And that is partly because it is cheap and requires little equipment. A friend of mine had a teacher tell him, "Do you know how many future NBA players are in my English class?"

And therein lies the rub. Most of those kids in the English class were not even on the high school team. They really thought that they were going to make it to the NBA? So there is a real fantasy and sense of unreality about the world that often exists amongst poor kids, especially poor black kids. It is somewhat understandable because they don't really have much besides their dreams. Nevertheless, one has to be careful in using basketball as a tool. Kids must be shown, taught, and mentored in other various aspects of life. Some of those things they may not want to hear. Such as, for example, excelling in school work. But it is important to teach leadership skills, banking, and finance, to create success outside the game of basketball, so they may be provide supported in all of their endeavors. If those things happen, then basketball as the tool, as the lure, will have performed the intended task.

Chapter Seven: Meeting My Wife/Starting a Family

"Those who love deeply never grow old: they may die of old age,

but they die young."

-Sir Arthur Wing Pinero

Eventually, I left the Chicago area and went to Kalamazoo, Michigan, as I had heard that I had some family there. One day, after living there for about six months, I was taking a bus to Western Michigan University to play some pick-up basketball. On the bus, I noticed two very fine young women. One was chocolate fine, while the other was caramel fine. Despite being an introvert, I still considered myself a lady's man. So, I was torn as to which one shall I start a conversation with. This played out in my mind for the entire bus ride, without any conversation actually taking place. That of itself may actually be some other indication or perhaps proof of my introversion.

By the end of the ride, I heard a voice in my ear that said that I should talk to the caramel fine young lady. So, I struck up a conversation and walked up to her in class, which took about thirty minutes. She told me that she had a boyfriend. Now, I'm thinking, why could she have not told me this sooner and saved our mutual time. Nevertheless, we enjoyed a good conversation, and I got her phone number. I informed her that we could be friends. And that ended our first meeting.

Later that day, I called her and asked what she was doing and if she wanted some company. She did. So, I went to see her. Once we were alone, I had this feeling that we were going to fall in love. It may not be love at first sight, but it was close. However, being the type of guy that I was, I also felt that we would soon be making love. So, time went by, and we saw each other every day, as it was becoming clear to me that I had supplanted her previous boyfriend. We were really hitting it off, and things were going well.

While our relationship grew and we were getting to know each other more, I was still in school at Western Michigan. At that time, back in March 2005, I was pursuing a career in fashion design under the major "Textile and Apparel Studies." This was my second year at Western. I was an above-average student; however, my focus soon shifted from academics to Calvin, as my grades began to slip. I was doing a minimum of classwork in order to pass my classes. I just wanted to get through the semester to summer, to a time where I would get a break from my studies, and my time with Calvin would be uninterrupted by homework and classes.

That summer seemed to fly by, and my apartment lease was about to end, and so was his. We were trying to figure out our living arrangements. Up to that point, we had been taking turns at staying at each other's apartment. I was still going to see my family every weekend because I was essentially a homebody and had a close-knit family. One weekend, after telling my family that I had been seeing someone for a while, I decided to bring him home with me.

I regularly took the Greyhound home because it was quick, about an hour on the bus to get home to Benton Harbor. I did not have a car, and neither did Calvin at this point, so we usually took public transportation as did many other college students in Kalamazoo.

I was quite nervous about this trip, being close to my family and wanting them to like him. My mother was easy going, and my little sister was protective of me, more like a big sister, while my father was always strict on my sibling and me, and that has always been his "love language." I was not sure how this visit was going to go and felt very uneasy. My sister proved hesitant to accept of Calvin. My mom and dad were observant of him, partly because they knew we had not been together long.

Due to our living arrangement, and my conscience, I started feeling guilty about us "shacking together," even though we each still had maintained our own apartments. Things were getting serious. We began to get pressure from my parents and other people, who cared about us, to make the right decision and consider "tying the knot" since we basically lived together. We were not quite ready to make that big of a move. So we continued to spend time together—a great deal of time.

In July of 2005, at the Taste of Chicago Festival, Calvin proposed at "Sharks," in Chicago. It was very romantic, and my answer was "yes." My mom and sister were with us on this trip but had gone to the bathroom just before he proposed. I was very excited about the possibility of this new adventure. But once I told my mom and my sister, what had happened while they were in the bathroom, they did not seem impressed. However, they tried to be happy because they knew that I was.

Time went on, and both our apartment leases were up around the beginning of September, and we were not sure where we would live. I came up with the idea of us moving in with my parents so that we could continue to be close to each other. I was, however, reluctant to ask my parents, but I did. They agreed to the arrangement which in our minds, was temporary. Prior to moving, we had obtained a car, Calving had not too good of credit, but had money to put down. He was working in Kalamazoo at Walmart and transferred his job to the South Haven Walmart. It was an overnight job. The Benton Harbor Walmart was not hiring at the time. I obtained a job at a community center and transferred to a fashion school in Chicago. With this new arrangement, I would catch the train, or Calvin would take me since he knew Chicago well.

I started school in September, and during that time, I also found out that I was pregnant with our first child, because I had been getting consistent morning sickness. I hid that from my dad because I knew he would be disappointed. I would get ready for school and even walk to the train station for most days, after throwing up. While going to school, working, and trying to come to terms with my pregnancy, the tension in the house began. I have started taking on the role of a wife cooking for my soon-to-be-husband, and my family was not quite happy about the progress of things. A family meeting was scheduled to discuss concerns in front of our pastors.

The meeting was held and provided everyone an opportunity to vent. However, it seemed we had only created more tension afterward because many issues remained unresolved. As a result, there was friction and animosity between my parents and Calvin. Things got even worse when I announced that I was pregnant. My dad was furious. His reaction was almost as if I was still a teenager in high school.

Now we faced even more pressure to get married. So, it was decided that after an upcoming Sunday church service, we would get married with the congregation serving as our guests. I wore a dress from a former pageant, while my bouquet and veil were donated by a family friend. Calvin bought his wedding ring and mine. The ceremony was officiated by my existing pastors.

We did not have a professional photographer, so my father offered to take pictures and videos, which we have since misplaced.

We did not have money for a honeymoon, so the pastors took up a love offering, which was used by us to secure a hotel room nearby, Michigan City, about a forty-five-minute drive. At the time, I was four months pregnant.

After the one-night honeymoon, we came back to my parents' home because we had not yet found our own place. I continued to work and go to school.

As time went on, the tension between Calvin and my parents increased. Calvin was not present a great deal, and this made matters worse with my parents. I was getting big and very close to giving birth. Finally, I gave birth to Calvin, Jr., in June, and we went back to my parents, still without our own place. In September, when our son was three months old, I was pregnant again. A month later, we found our own apartment, a small one, in a town nearby.

We moved in just before Thanksgiving, and my sister moved in with us. This was because we had agreed that Calvin would be off to follow his dream of playing basketball. This meant he would only come home on the weekends, and even then, not every weekend.

Around the time of our first anniversary, Calvin, my sister, and I got into a big fight. Calvin was upset because he felt that my sister and I were ungrateful about his hard work and determination to provide for us. The argument was very heated, and Calvin threw my clothes and other belongings down the stairs. Calvin Jr. was shaking because of the noise, and the entire apartment building had probably heard us. I called my father and went there to stay that night, ultimately moving back. Finally, Calvin and I made peace, and he was welcomed back at my parents' home on weekends.

Sometime later, my dad and Calvin got into another huge fight one day, over Calvin not taking off his dirty work shoes at the house. The fight got ugly, and my dad was in his room, loading his gun. I told my dad that we were leaving. Shortly after this, my sister got an apartment with her boyfriend, and I moved in with them. Calvin joined us on the weekends. He never stayed for long. I eventually quit school and began to look for another job.

Over the next few years, we stayed with relatives on and off in different states, such as Arkansas, Michigan, and Indiana. This was not good for our marriage, and tension was usually present. We had established a pattern, after that first major argument on our anniversary, of having huge arguments each year around the same time as our anniversary. This continued for several anniversaries. Many of our problems had to do with our different perspectives on life. We began to wonder if we would make it as a married couple.

Between 2010 and 2017, we experienced many transitions and many losses in our lives. Calvin's mother died, and then my great grandmother, to whom I was very close, passed away. Calvin and I both lost our jobs. One job I lost paid well and was a professional postilion, at an advanced level and with many benefits. However, it was quite stressful. I also had lost a car and had to pick up the pieces of a failed business.

Some positives took place in 2009. I started to go back to school, more focused this time and completed a degree in Early Childhood Education in just three years. Calvin had encouraged me to open my own home daycare back in 2009, along with attending school. By the time I graduated in 2012, I was getting good jobs, with better pay and benefits. Along the line, Calvin had stopped his pursuit of basketball and worked a variety of jobs.

In 2013, things again went bad between us, and we began to discuss a divorce. There had occurred some infidelity as a result of us being "emotionally done," with our marriage. Still, we remained tenuously together, but in 2015 there was again an instance of infidelity rooted in bitterness.

In 2016 we lost our house and moved in back with family. Despite earlier positives, we again almost called it "quits." I even went to see a family attorney, to get things done in order, for divorce. We just had so much frustration and resentment between us. Still, we held on. I do not know how, but we did.

In 2017, things took a turn in quite a positive direction. I got a good job at a local daycare and started to graduate school, with a scholarship covering 95% of my tuition. Calvin joined an energy company that allowed him to be his own boss. In a matter of months, he advanced to an executive level. Last but not least, we renewed our commitment to each other, to our marriage, and family (I neglected to mention the birth of our daughter, Leaha, earlier in my account. She is a year behind Calvin, Jr. in school. Both are excellent students and great kids!). We decided that with all that we had gone through, and the fact that we still stood tall, we should be able to make it going forward. There was a renewed assurance of our future together.

Since we made that commitment to each other, in 2017, we have enjoyed the best years of our marriage and our best years professionally. This includes the opening of my own daycare business and me securing a graduate degree. Sometimes it just takes a while to get things right, but perseverance can pay off.

LaDawn White Swan

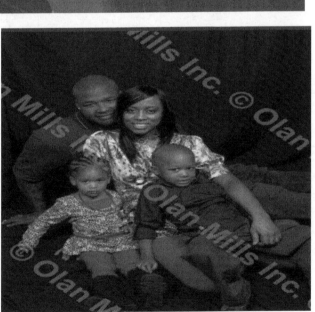

Chapter Eight: Energy Executive/Introspection

"Although the world is full of suffering, it is also full of overcoming it."

-Helen Keller

One day I was selling pots and pans, door to door in Granger, Indiana. A guy was watching me from a tanning salon and came out to speak to me. He asked if I knew anything about energy deregulation, and I told him that I did not. He told me to meet him at McDonald's around noon. I did, and we watched a 15-minute video. Before the video even ended, I was hooked and ready to sign on. As I have said elsewhere, I am a natural salesman, and that type of work appeals to me because I can determine my own level of success and not have a boss all over me all day long. As a salesman, I am very motivated (you have to be if you are selling pots and pans door to door).

The deregulated energy business is primarily in gas and electric utilities. It is a multi-layered sales operation. For example, I sign up and get say, 15 people, to sign up. And then they work to sign other people. The system sounds like a scam or a pyramid scheme, but it is not actually. It works and is completely legal and completely a boon to those who want to save money on energy bills. People can easily save up to

70% on their household energy bills while maintaining the same supplier. Of course, the suppliers, or other huge energy companies, do not want anyone to know of this. They put some "hidden" costs on your household gas bill, for example, which can be overcome by signing up with an energy provider for the deregulated services. You have to then be charged less. Again, it sounds too good to be true, but it really is the result of Congressional legislation, deregulating the energy giants.

I told him that I was looking for a good friendship and that it is not all about money with me. Money comes and goes, but good friends last forever. I think this shocked the gentleman. Jason was his name. At any rate, I paid $101.60 to sign up. I knew I was going to be successful, but I did not boast predictions about it. I knew my actions would speak the loudest. So, I took everything that I learned from selling drugs and observing people. Very quickly, my style of network marketing moved forward with great success. Money was coming in, and I was attracting attention in the field.

While I was working hard, I was also helping others get started in the deregulation energy business. Maybe I was helping people too much because once I backed off a bit, some of them stopped working. It was all fine while I was doing the work, but they were not matching my efforts. Some people began to get envious of my success, not seeing the effort and the planning that I had put into the business. I felt they did not want to see me succeed. But I was not about to let anyone stop my progress.

I started to go state to state doing business. Most of that time, I was living in my car and showering at gyms after workouts—a pattern similar to my drug-selling days. I met different people every day while doing business. I was networking, I signed people up and established friendships—some proved good, some did not. But always, I treated people with respect.

There are over 500,000 consultants in this business and maybe 150 executives and around 35 national consultants. Here I was, the guy who grew up with no parents and lived in the system, attended six different high schools, had no college degree, but had become hugely successful— and quick. I soon had over 3,000 customers. I did it fast, in fact, virtually faster than any other person in the country.

So I made a lot of money fast. I met some very "high-up" executives and attracted to them by my rapid number of sales. They took me under their wing and showed me much about business, which proved to be eye-opening for me. I learned the good and the bad. I learned about integrity and corruption. I had helped many people, giving some of them money. But still, I sensed a great deal of hate and jealousy directed towards me.

Eventually, actually, quite quickly, I was recognized for my efforts. I had become an executive in the business. At one point, I was working out of an office in Manhattan in the same building as former President Bill Clinton had his office. I was flying all over the country, talking to different people, doing workshops, and so forth. And I was called to Dallas to receive an award from the company headquarters.

During the time that I worked in New York, a friend got me involved with some heavy hitters in the motivational speaking world. I found myself serving as bodyguard one night at Carnegie Hall, to Bob Proctor, Les Brown, and Rev. Michael Beckwith. My friend is actually the right-hand man of Bob Proctor, and so I had been to Bob's house and been around him a little bit. I had no idea who he was until much later. He is a nice gentleman, and I can say that I enjoyed this little detour, in my business education, to take care of, and hear the motivational speakers, that I described. I have never been one to be unduly impressed with fame and fortune, not being a name-dropper, but when I found out how famous some of the people I had met in New York were, I was surprised, to say the least.

As my family became more and more financially secure, I started to feel that the business world was, in many ways, much worse than the drug-dealing world. I just seldom do things for the money. I really need or care about it, only enough to live on. The backbiting, jealousy, and other negatives of the business world began to weigh on me.

Life is a funny thing for many people. We go about our everyday business and get so busy, so caught up in detail, whether at work or at home, that we forget to stop and take a moment to breathe. Everything is fast-paced, full speed ahead. We may think we know where we are headed, but when we get there, it is never enough, while we move towards our next shallow goal. We forget to think about what is really going on inside of us. Everything is external. And before long, we've grown old and wasted a great deal of personal potential, as far as developing as human beings.

A part of this is just our fast-paced society, but also, an important part is our quest for the almighty dollar. In my case, it was a quest for survival when I was younger, and then the quest was changed to focus on my family when I got married and had children. I was constantly obsessed with where the next dollar would come from to feed and clothe my family.

I decided to take some time off (As I had money coming in, more than enough for my family to live on) and did not really need to work for some while. I wanted to work on myself, and maybe to see what God really wanted me to be doing. My success in the energy field now had allowed me to back off and examine who I was. What I saw were habits and thoughts I did not deem worth keeping, something I had never taken time for introspection, never assessed my morality, my integrity, nor my humanity. I had not read books and been exposed to concepts of improving oneself as a person. What was my purpose in life? Why had I been spared, all those years ago, when that gun misfired, I was knocked out instead of being shot. Maybe even the proverbial "meaning of life."

I went with a friend, in the energy business to Spain. I found the weather to be great and the country to be delightfully peaceful, happy, and non-racist. Life's pace was very different from that of the United States. I loved the people, they were always smiling, always friendly towards me. I started taking some time to think and meditate. I pondered questions such as, "What is really important in life?" I began thinking about people that I admired, as well as those I did not like well. What was the difference? I thought about the people that I knew who did nothing but cover or justify their behavior with religion and/or materialism. I thought about people who were condescending or completely intolerant of the views or lifestyles of others if those things did not agree with the way that they lived their lives.

I began to realize that I was not the person I wanted to be and that some things were there that upset me within my marriage, which I had blamed on LaDawn, which was just as much my of doing as hers. I had often thought that her family was too involved in our married life. I also felt that her first allegiance was to them and not me. In retrospect, while some of that may have been true, there has also been some unconscious jealousy as she had a close-knitted family, where I had no family at all and simply could not relate to her relationship with them. (As a result of me working on myself, our marriage has gotten much stronger. We

72

support each other in many ways, not the least of which is professional. We are partners. I never wanted to allow my marriage to break up or create a hole in the family like I experienced as a child. I have to keep working at everything in my life, but especially my family. They have to come first always. It took me a long time to arrive where I am today. But, back to Spain...)

I began to understand my responsibility as my life unfolded, and I could see other explanations for my problems. I began to see the possibility of becoming a better version of myself.

I started playing basketball, getting in shape, and worked out with professional teams. Eventually, I started doing voluntary work with kids, centered towards basketball. These kids are ones who had tough beginnings in life, just as I had. I rediscovered what I had always known about my purpose in life, and why I was put onto earth. Working with kids ignited a passion within me. I began to feel less uptight and more relaxed. I was happier with myself, as well as more content in my thoughts. It was tough to think of going back to the U.S. as I wanted no more part in the rat race. I had a higher calling, personally and professionally.

Once back in the United States, I started to fall back into my old habits, and my "hurry up" lifestyle. Then in a few months, the pandemic started, everything slowed down, and suddenly, I was back with my thoughts from Spain. I began to slow down, to read, to talk to friends about the subjects that I have been discussing here. I vowed to continue my quest to be a better person. I got inside of my head, took responsibility for all my shortcomings, and for many things that I had blamed on others before. I reached a point of peace with myself, knowing I would continue to work towards being a better person. I hope I never lose this fervor to live in the moment, taking time for what is important in life.

Chapter Nine: My Vision and Starting a Non-Profit

"Every individual matters, be it non-human or human. Every individual has a role to play. Every individual may make a difference. We cannot live a single day without trying to make an impact on the world around us. And we have free choice—what sort of difference do we want to make? Do we want to make the world around us a better place? Or not? "-Jane Goodall

When I was around ten years old, my caseworker asked me what I wanted to do when I was older. I told her that I wanted to work with kids, but did not know how or in what fashion. I did not want kids to experience what I had experienced, no parents, no money, no food, abuse, and so on.

At this time, I was troubled and began asking God why these things had happened to me, and if I did anything wrong to cause them. I asked why my parents didn't come for me, why I didn't have a family, when am I going to get a family? The mind of a child cannot always perceive everything that is missing, but some things, like parents, are sort of instinctive.

And so, my purpose in life really has been in my head for a long time. I just did not know how to get it out into a plan. But now, I know what I want to do. I want to open up programs and facilities where kids can get food and clothes, where they can shower, and, if necessary, sleep. I want them to be safe and be coached and mentored. I want them to experience sports. I want them to feel successful and feel loved.

I want to guide these kids, counsel them, coach them, and help them grow into productive citizens. I do not want to do it for any money. I want to do it because this is what these kids deserve in their lives. I want to keep them out of jail, help them find jobs, and give them a chance for success. This has been my reason for being on earth all along. And now, I know it in certainty.

Fair disclosure here, I had, for years, expressed a desire to work with kids. I trained some in basketball and coached basketball in schools. But there was something in the back of my mind, something that needed to be expanded upon. When I was in Spain, all this began to crystallize into something very definite.

So I started a 501c-3 charitable company called Euro Hoopz. I suppose I chose this name because of my experience in Spain, but also because I know that many poor little black kids aspire to be a part of the NBA or WNBA, and if that does not work out, they want to play basketball in Europe. I began looking for like-minded people to help me fulfill this dream.

I needed a strong team, people with passion, people with skills, and a caring attitude. To this end, I have sought out such people for my board. They come from a variety of professions and have all something to offer kids. I am still looking for others, but I am very happy with the Board that we have assembled.

Initially, the beginning program that we have laid out will consist of some travel basketball teams and open gym programs, a soccer league, a leadership class, tutoring and study skills education, and lastly, a micro-business component that I hope leads to some entrepreneurship opportunities, allowing the kids to make money. Making money, even for young kids, may keep them from stealing and dealing. From there, it is my fervent hope that our modest beginnings grow into the vision described above. We will run this program starting on the west side of South Bend in with two Catholic school parishes, as an after school program. We will fund it with grants and donations and also have some paid staff acquired from local high schools and colleges.

Our partnership with these Catholic parishes is the product of my friendship with the pastor, Father Glenn Kohrman. He is a wonderful human being, and has believed in me and helped me since the day I met him---and I am not even a member of his parish. He sees a need for a program for his schools, especially for St. John's, a poor school, that until recently, had declining enrollment. It now seems that Father and his principal, Brian Carver, have begun to turn things around. By our 501c-

3 taking over the after-school program in the fall of 2020, it is our sincere hope that we can help the enrollment some more, mostly to fill a void in the lives of these children, who are exactly our targeted group.

To that end, I began coaching girls' basketball at St. John's during the 2019-20 season. It is a fledgling program with only eight or nine girls, but I have utter confidence that within a few short years, we will be doing some great things.

Beyond our initiation, I envision a program that will grow into other parts of the city and will expand its offerings, to better serve the youth in need. I have already had discussions with my caseworkers and executives from my former group home in Chicago, seeking their advice and wisdom. We hope to use some of their programming ideas, and in all likelihood, they will replicate some of ours. Maybe one day, we will even create a joint partnership in an area or another.

It is frankly, also in the back of my mind, but never far from my thoughts that someday we may expand to Europe or elsewhere in the world. South America could most definitely use us. Asia is starting to play more and more basketball now more than ever. But the first country that comes to mind is Spain. This is clearly a result of my positive visit there in the summer of 2019. That visit set my course in life, once and for all. Those kids that I worked with changed my life and gave me clarity.

Epilogue

A man, after he has brushed off the dust and chips of his life, will

have left only the hard, clean questions:

Was it good, or was it evil?

Have I done well—or ill?

-John Steinbeck

In the epilogue, I would like to touch upon a variety of topics that may not have completely come to light in the body of this book. I suppose much will be miscellaneous or random thoughts, but I want to put them out here so that people will better understand where I come from and what I am attempting to accomplish. And, in the process, people will better understand me and what my views are for the future. In a way, I suppose these are items which make up a portion of my personal philosophy on life.

First, let me say that it is somewhat audacious for a person who has probably only read a singular book in his life, to actually write of one. But I truly, believe I have a story to tell one that is unique because I came out of my environment against 98% odds that consumed my peers. The fact is, I could be making big money right now, today, as a drug dealer. But instead, somewhere along the line, I learned that money is not everything there is. As I have relayed elsewhere, I only need enough money for my family and I to live, I do not worship money or the pursuit of it thereof. I do value friendship and loyalty. Somewhere along the line, I developed morality. I learned to care for others, a great deal more than any care that I experienced in my earliest life. I changed, many people do not. I have compassion for others. Above all, I want to see that kids not replicating my early life. Every child deserves a better fate.

Nevertheless, for years my friends, those who had known of my story, have encouraged my writing of this book. One friend told me that writing a book brings instant credibility to a certain person. He told me that maybe things should not be that way, but they are and writing a book has created many experts, I hope he is correct. My intention is to get my story out there so that I can generate the resources I need to help kids. It is evident that the government, schools, community, philanthropic groups, and community centers are not meeting the entire requirement. Young black kids still get in trouble, still do not have enough food, have no support, and as just one example, still know nothing about money, taxes, banking, insurance, and all the adult skills needed to live successfully. They start way behind the average middle or upper-middle-class kid and fail to catch up.

I would now like to express some thoughts about religion in general. I did not grow up in any religion. I knew only a little bit from my father's mother, as I have mentioned earlier. At various times in my teen years and early adult years, I had minimal exposure to Christianity. Once I got married, I attended church with my wife, LaDawn, because she and her family are Christians. However, it really did not seem to be a fit for me. I have noticed what I feel is a predisposition of many great Christians to judge other people and to insist that their ways of worship are the only true way. That really turns me off.

When I met Father Glenn, I thought about becoming a Catholic. He is such a great example of a person living his faith. But I noticed I was the only black person who attended mass. That made me a bit uncomfortable.

But I was definitely a searcher, someone feeling that there must be a God and that there must be a plan for me and my life. So, I guess you could say that it was a belief deep within myself that I was not experiencing an organized religion that felt right for me, or in which I felt completely at home.

Ultimately, I met people from many different religions, including Muslims and Buddhists. People from Spain, India, China, various African countries, and Cambodia. I liked the way that they treated me and the way that they reflect on all the people that they met. Their daily interactions seemed to me to was to endorse their religious views. They, like Father Glenn, seemed to be truly good and admirable people. They never judge and never put their religion out there to me as the one true religion. I became fast friends with many of these individuals before I ever knew what religion they belonged too.

Because I titled this book, *Faith of An Unwanted Child*, I hope that at least some get the hint of my faith has come through in the telling of my story. Initially, as a young child, and through my teenage years, my faith was indeed in myself. It had to be. I had no one else to look up to. At least, no people to depend upon. And yet, even then, I think that on some level, there was a belief, a spark deep inside of me that made me feel that somehow God was within me. A belief that somehow God would eventually guide me to some sense of security, to some sense of normalcy which I had never known of, and to understand the purpose of my life.

With the above said, I am sure that the reader understands that metaphysical concepts such as faith, are not always easy for a young child. They are made even less so in the case of a child who grows up in such uncertain circumstances and conditions as did my siblings and I. And yet, with that said, I cannot help but feel that there is an innate, if often unexpressed, faith that exists within a child, in all children. In the end, though they cannot verbalize it, perhaps that undefined faith is all that they really have. And just because it may not be verbalized does not make it any less real. Faith is felt, it is known to be there, somewhere deep within. It can have a sort of sustaining power, even in the darkest of circumstances.

Based on my life experiences, the people I have met, the people I have observed, and what mind my tells me is right, I have developed certain general and specific views about religion and faith. My specific faith or views I will leave for another time. But I can say that in broadly general terms, I believe that all religions are about trying to have or create a good heart and to live a good life, helping others, and never judging ("lest ye be judged"). Some people seem to achieve these goals better than others, but that is all part of the human being's experience. I believe that faith is deeply personal, not always easy to express, and difficult to describe, but very real, nonetheless. Without faith, what do we really have? What is there to comfort and sustain us?

To live a life of faith, I intend to help others whenever possible, to live a life of integrity and decency, to have moral values, and to continue to seek the voice of God, in all the many ways that he expresses himself in my life.

I would like to make a few comments about race. I have a very good friend who's white. He once told me that I did not seem to have any racial prejudice. He thought that it was remarkable considering the occurred events of my life, the places I grew up, and the fact that I had recently been put in jail overnight, by a white police officer and judge. I did not have a Michigan driver's license on me (At that time, I had an Illinois driver's license, but I did not have it with me) back when I was pulled over for speeding. He knew that this last incident was nothing but

86

the sheer outcome of racism, what some would call systemic racism or profiling. And it was indeed. But it was also "local" racism, that is, racism that exists within a particular geographic locale.

The problem with racism is that it vilifies a person based simply on the color of their skin, and maybe some times worn stereotypes. I simply cannot operate that way. I have had people of all races help me or show me an act of kindness. I guess I have had people of many races have caused me pain, real or perceived. In my mind, people are just people. The color of the skin is not a factor with me. I was not taught nor, did I learn to hate white people, even though I grew up with very few whites in my environment.

There is no question about white racism and white nationalism being on the rise again in recent years. A fact that is hard to reconcile with in the year 2020. At a time when persons from every race ought to have equal opportunities, we are still dealing with ignorance in this regard. Some people think it has gone away, but that is not so. Racism may be more subtle now, harder to detect, yet it is instilled amongst many of us.

A white mentor of mine once simplified his views on racists in the United States by saying that such individuals only recognize two types of people, dumb niggers and smart niggers, or dumb crackers and smart crackers. This, of course, points out that there are white racists and there are black racists. His point being that a racist mind is so concretely set from the beginning, that there really is no dealing with them. Perhaps racism will never go away. In the United States, the difference in racists is really about power. Clearly, the white racists have more power, and so white racism is more pervasive and destructive than what black racists are able to accomplish with an agenda they may have.

And finally, whether we are talking about outright racism, poverty, social justice, or inequality, make no mistake; this is not a level playing field. Non-white children, as a group, face more challenges and obstacles in their lives than do white children

My Parents:

My mother died from HIV after a sad life full of drug abuse. I never got to say, "Goodbye." But for all that I had been through, as a product of her neglect, she was still my mother, and those bonds always remain in one fashion or another.

My father is still alive, I have seen him a few times and have introduced him to his grandchildren. I hope that his life is better now. He and I are not close, and we will never be, but he is my father the same way my mother is. I have had other men in my life who have been much more like fathers to me. But to be fair, I do not know all that he went through or what led him to the path he chose for life.

If I internalized one message, or a lesson, from my parents, it would be not to do to my children what they did to me by neglect. I intend to be a real father, while they have a great mother, in my wife, LaDawn.

They will never have to experience what my siblings and I had to. I have a family now, and that means a great deal to me. But I also have to learn to be a parent, because I never really had parents to set an example of what parents should be like.

It has been suggested that perhaps I ought to write a letter to my deceased mother, as a process of healing. This is a technique that I understand is sometimes used in psychotherapy. And perhaps, I should even put my thoughts down in a letter to my father. He is still alive, and I could choose to either send it to him or not. But at the very least, it puts my emotions and thoughts into written words, which of themselves are a powerful tool.

Below is my effort to address my mother and my father individually.

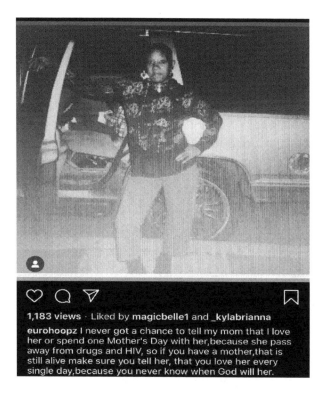

Dear Mama,

You died so young, and I am so sorry. I never got to say good-bye.

But surely you realize that is mostly your fault, you were never around.

I was only a child. I needed you. I wanted to be held and to be loved. When those things did not happen, I was very angry with you. Sometimes I blamed myself. What had I done wrong? Was I bad? Why did you not love me enough to come around?

You will be happy to know that I took care of my sisters whenever I could. Because we did not have you or daddy, we knew that we had to care for each other. I hope that makes you proud.

I am a grown man now. I have a family with a wonderful wife and two teenage children. I am doing my very best to be a good man.

Momma, I love you, and I forgive you. I now know you did the best that you could under the circumstances. Mommas are special to children, and you will always be my momma!

Love,

Calvin.

Maybe now, as an adult, I understand my mother better. I have certainly seen what drugs do to people and how out of control they become. I do forgive her, but there will always be an empty void in my heart that should have been filled with more memories of my momma. But for all of that, I love my momma.

Dear Dad,

I have spent a great deal of time in my life being angry at you. You were rarely there for me, and when you were, all we did was fight. I now know that it was my fault, as much or more than yours. I wanted to be free like I had been before, while you wanted to discipline me as a father. I was not used to that. I was also angry that I was poor, and you never gave me things or provided for the girls and I, the way that fathers are supposed to do.

One thing is for sure, you showed me by example what I did not want to be. I did not want to be a gang-banger, to get shot, or to ever be sent to prison. And I want you to know that I have not done any of those things.

You have met my family. I do not understand why you do not try to be more involved with us. Nevertheless, I provide for them in a way I never experienced as a child. My family is a blessing to me. I am thankful that I never had to walk in your shoes. I forgive you, I wish you peace, and that the rest of your life will be trouble-free.

Calvin

I cannot sign the letter to my father, with "love," because I feel numb about him, in general. He has had and still has the opportunity to be a part of my life, but he chooses not to for whatever reason. In that regard, he is treating his grandchildren somewhat like he treated me, which is to say, not treating them at all. Still, he is my father, and I do not hate him. In the end, maybe his life, and the trouble he got into, really was an example that saved me.

And so, I have started Euro Hoopz, for reasons explained earlier. We are a fledgling organization, but one that I am determined to make successful. Below is our first brochure describing our current programs.

Finally, let me say that if the reader would like me to come to your organization as a guest speaker, or to motivate your staff, I am available. This is what I do.

Likewise, if anyone would like to help our program as a volunteer or an intern, or just in donating money, we welcome your help.

We can be contacted at:
Euro Hoopz 417 S 27TH ST SOUTH BEND, IN 46615-2742
Or, contact me directly at:
calvinswan@eurohoopz.net
Phone: (614) 202-5842

Acknowledgments

"At times our own light goes out and is rekindled by a spark from another person. Each of us has cause to think with deep gratitude of those who have lighted the flame within us."

-Albert Schweitzer

Typically, when someone writes a book, they have a section of acknowledgments, thanking all the people who helped to make this book possible. I am going to take it a step further and use this opportunity to thank the people in my life who have made the greatest difference for me:

My wife, La Dawn, you have loved me all these years and have given me two beautiful and awesome children. I know it has not been easy, and I know I may be difficult at times. Thank you, I love you so much! I know I do not tell you often how much you mean to me. You are my partner, my love, my indispensable other.

Kirby Whitacre, you have been like a father to me for many years. You have always been there for me, no matter what time of day or night, helped me with everything, and mentoring me in life and decision-making. Thank you, and I love you.

P.J., I want to thank you for helping me to learn about business and introducing me to some great people, many of them famous. You have shown me a totally different world from which I had previously experienced, and you have been a big brother to me.

Father Glenn, you believed in me, you have shared my vision and passion for working with children and youth. You were always there, no matter what, helping with my kids' Christmas gifts, and talking with me, taking my "urgent" calls, and being my sounding board. You have helped with me starting this program. You do not just preach the word; you live it through your actions.

Jeff Meixel, I want to thank you for always being there for me since the very first day I moved to South Bend. You taught me about basketball programs and gave me the opportunity to train your daughter. You helped me to get my first coaching job at middle school. Thank you for also being a Father figure to me.

Jason Jenkins, you have always been there for me since the very first day that we met, and you spoke with me about Ambit Energy. Thank you for being a brother to me. I can talk to you about anything. Thank you for never changing on me, even when others did. Thanks for everything. I love you.

One risks leaving out someone or multiple someone(s) when attempting to recount those who have meant so much, and done so much to help. And one risks forgetting those people, whose names are unknown, and who were often complete strangers, who on one or more occasions, committed acts of kindness or help towards me. I apologize, I may not know your names, but your kindness has made a difference. It is for all of you that I pass it along, play it forward whenever I can.

Thank you for reading this. I really appreciate your time in reading my story.

A word from those we helped

I have had a wonderful time with Mr. Swan in his facility. I wanted to play basketball since, like forever, but never got enough playtime in school. I would go play with the older kids outdoor, but they were into some other stuff that I was not into. My mother did not like me playing with those boys, and honestly, neither did I. Going to the facility every day after school has helped me make new friends, who are just like me. We eat together, play together, and have fun. We train every day in the open gym, go through various drills, and then play some games. I play basketball while others play soccer. I have gone very well at playing basketball, as noticed by my school friends and coach. It is because of the extra training I have been getting whilst so many good people. I really appreciate Mr. Swans as he has been there for us every step of the way. My mother works as a nanny and does not make much, but Mr. Swan took as his facility did not ask of any fees. He often told us of the many people that donated to his cause and taught us the value of appreciation. **– Edward McCarthy**

***

I don't enjoy school so much. I guess I overall have a bad time at school as I'm not so good at communicating with people. Most kids are mean, and I do not know why. I'm not like them, and my mother always says that I'm good, and to never be like those other kids. I try to play with them, but they always pick one me and make fun of me. I really want to play soccer. My favorite player is Griffin Dorsey. I wanted to be like him. My friend was going to a place and always talked about how I should come, he played their often. He was an orphan like me. When I went there, they were so nice to me and offered me food to eat. I was mostly hungry when I came back from school because my mother would usually cook enough for us to eat dinner only. We are poor. But know I go to euro hoopz every day, after school, and play. The kids here are so nice, and everyone is just so helpful. My mother is really happy that I have been making new friends. There is no fee here, and it runs on donations. Many poor kids from my school have joined, and they have even received donations from our school too. –Ian Norton

***

I grew up with an abusive father who abused my mother and me. He was a convict and soon fled the country, which left me abandoned at an adoption facility. I had many friends, and we smoked weed often. Sometimes one of the boys would get some coke and crack, and we would get high and cause havoc. I used to feel happy and did not care much for anything else. I saw sports on the TV and imagined being like them. The crowd cheering for them, chanting their name; that was something that felt good to me, but I could not play any sports, and even at school, I was the worst of them all. I was a though black kid, so no one was able to bully me, but no one wanted to be my friend either. Euro hoopz helped me get strong. They gave me good food to eat, and also taught me what it meant to have a good circle around me. I'm proud to say that I'm no longer doing drugs or having a bad circle around me. I would really ask everyone who reads this to donate to Mr. Swan's facility, he is changing the lives of so many like me - **Kevin Jones**

"Let's join hands and help those who need it. Helping one person is equal to helping humanity. The world has already witnessed many sad stories. Let's hear the happy ones."

-Calvin Swan